Oubliette

Oubliette

Poems by

Peter Richards

Verse Press
Amherst, MA

Published by Verse Press

Copyright © 2001 by Peter Richards

Library of Congress Cataloging-in-Publication Data
Richards, Peter, 1967-
  Oubliette / Peter Richards.— 1st ed.
     p. cm.
  ISBN 0-9703672-2-8 (pbk. : alk. paper)
  I. Title.
  PS3563.E3459 T47 2000
  811'.54—dc21
                                    00-011568

Set in Electra

Designed by Brian Henry

Printed in the United States of America

9 8 7 6 5 4 3 2 1

FIRST EDITION

www.versepress.org

for Susa

Acknowledgments

Grateful acknowledgement is made to the editors of the journals in which these poems first appeared: *Agni*: "The Sea Looking On." *Colorado Review*: "The Blue Nest," "On the Conditions Presently Needed," "Not Taking Place," "The Bird Maker's Last," "Rose Maker's Fever." *Denver Quarterly*: "Because There is No Soft." *Harvard Review*: "Suicide's Last Week at a Glance," "Castrovalva," "The Drawstring Hisses." *The Iowa Review*: "Elegy for Music," "Dawn." *Island* (Australia): "Hornet." *The Massachusetts Review*: "Circled Square Drawn to Scale," "Boy for Sale." *Meanjin* (Australia): "On the Dangers of Not Reading Aloud," "This is the Color," "*Paradise*: Directions for Reading." *Norwattuk*: "The Moon is a Moon." *Slope* (www.slope.org): "Which Oval her Ministry," "Warning Bretagne," "A Third Tree." *Verse*: "Oubliette," "Remainder," "Unable," "Bulrushes," "My Death Bed of Flowers," "Siphons," "In Between Jed and Yeul," "Dear Uriah," "The Fourth Book of Nathan." *Westerly* (Australia): "Nettles."

Thanks to the Massachusetts Cultural Council for financial support. Special thanks to Brian Henry for selecting the order in which these poems appear. Thanks to my family, friends, and teachers for their love and guidance while writing this book.

Table of Contents

Introduction

It is better to be a new young god in American Poetry than to be President of the United States. It is the only divine *and* democratic position available. There are not many such places in human history. I do believe this with my whole being. I'm also positive this insight comes from the depth and destiny of American poetry. Poetry rules, makes you fresh, "when I blur my eyes and wiggle my tongue," *produces* hope, power, insight, delight, joy, awe, meaning, new technologies, mutations and the most important protection. We know we need it with our genes stitched and pushed around. And billions of dollars shining in broken mirrors. Money is blind, poetry is not. Language stores our salvation and the place where it happens is in the blank page touched by the hand of the new poet.

So when I was given *Oubliette* in 1998 I needed only three pages and I was dismantled, washed, seduced, fresh (me too), young (me too), charmed, gentle, full of joy. I remember it happened a few days before flying to read in Tucson, and once there, I was unable to talk about anything else but *Oubliette*. I got immense power from the manuscript and poured it over the students. I was deeply moved and flooded by the grace of it. I needed to share it in the desert with people there. I sensed *Oubliette* must be famous by circling around in secret ways—I knew I could not be the only one to know about its powers. It's a mystery to me why this book was not taken *immediately*. Did we all want to drink from it secretly?

As a European I came to this country many times tired, full of melancholy, old. In the last three years *Oubliette* kept me alive (if I had the force to be open to it, not always, sometimes you want to bury your highest moments, to deny them). I still don't know what's in the book and don't want to know. I just jump in it, get blessed,

store it somewhere deep down or high up, or on the skin, or in
the heart.

> Imagine something strictly forbidden.
> Now this same thing suddenly
> sanctioned, involving your tongue.

It is inscrutable how Peter Richards produces this religious magma
and bathes himself and us in it. How he restores internal time to
the work of art. I don't know and I don't want to tell you about it.

Get wet by yourself.

— TOMAZ SALAMUN

Oubliette

Remainder

I am not broken as they envision, am not partial,
porous, nor will I grind into hopes pestle held.
In so many ways I shame impact.
On impact, I lie about the stars burning gently.
I lie about Forgiveness, and with my head on her lap,
lie about the azaleas I saw printed inside.
Long before thumbs, happenstance
must have patched me together.
In that, I sometimes fear I am deathless—
fear for now on I'll serve as the points
upon which various and misguided winds
can agree. They agree I'm afraid
and that fears will keep them safe.
Some blow a head full of caution they want me to feign.
Some land with occupants they wish I could hold.
Still others come discharging a Mary they insist I intake.
But I fear there is no carriage to begin with,
nor place to be inside of. No sooner do I arrive
than I find this or that is already full.
More recently I'm afraid of the linnets.
I fear for the palatine comfort in their still-day song.

Unable

In the garden behind the garden
a birdbath swallows all the birds.

Rising above it,
their ghosts think *leaves,*
submerged and shrunken.

The stasis between wing beats
resents such a pause.
Today it paused itself into being.

Or the bath was placed here
by nostalgia for birds —

when all the odes
suddenly turned carnivorous,
not for the song,
but for the ones who sang it.

Or I've just grown tired of watching this pool.
Tired of the swallow
that soars in the depths below.

When I drank from these waters
I drank from my own face —

an endless wet bird
rose in my throat,
at once wingless
and unable to sing.

The Hood

I make a great bird of prey in the ground
ascending in circles that weaken the floor.
One eye is keen and peers up past the bore
drilled by the other. Shy with my circle
I went down hooded before it was mine—
saw a whole flock of me alight on the earth
and the great bird of prey was the hood I see.

The Blue Nest

Inquiry exerts their nest.

In the beginning the nest turned blue
around its edges. Even the grasses,
the sprigs, and what few strands of latent
(cut the night before from the girls,
still too young to be girls) turned a milky
blue in advance for the nest, in advance
for my peering down from the branches.

It's hard to tell how lovers get along in the day.
In the day they find it hard to think up a nest.

Try patiently scraping your trowel
along the clover's tender shoots.
Try a few grains of the powder
that fall into your hand.

Imagine something strictly forbidden.
Now this same thing suddenly
sanctioned, involving your tongue.

This is what it's like when I bend—
when I blur my eyes and wiggle my tongue
slow and soft along the roots.

When they finally lay sleeping
I crept down from my ambuscade
and carefully wrapped their blueness in paper.

It is the same paper you're holding it now.

My Death Bed of Flowers

The Some-whats have come to persuade me.
They drag three gowns unfolding my Mass face—
the drawstring ravels *no ashes at all* ...
The Some-whats have come to convey me.
Waters are tepid, careful, and I walk on the waters—
a pond with your name drank from these woods.

With their long and lute fed black sponge of hair
the Some-whats are bending to bathe me—
a trickle of three days for the back of my neck,
a night once known and not how it seems
washes what washes away,
all but the last things washing away.

I'm told to crawl inside and leave those hoods behind.
I'm told to lie quiet—pretending is good.
Among these there's a petal that's you.
I bend for the petal that's me.
Find each petal bending for me.

I say "pretty." I'm allowed to say pretty.
It tickles, this hill. This sprinkle of flowers.
This all-along-a-hill slow bending for me.

Carillon

Beneath some bells, one glanced over me
with a mouthful of speechless cold.
If sparks leach their way into the rim,
these too had been blackened by cold.
It was if cold were sequestered
by all the other bells.

I want to show you the cylinder it heaves
for taking me in. I'm in this room
and that bell is far away.
I have no choice but to tell you how I was living.
But I'm still here, I can even record
things that you point to.

You point at the brown leaf with its fleck of red.
Still, I insist on showing you that cylinder,
for if you don't see,
if you don't see this black fluted tube
inviting me into the bell, it won't
be as though cold had taken me in.

Suicide's Last Week at a Glance

On Monday the black X in the Sunday box is the eye of a
    cartoon walrus.
Perhaps an anvil crushed its skull,
or the penguin's poison caused his lungs to freeze.

On Tuesday the black X in the Sunday box is tenth on the list
    of tiny sounds.
For seven he hears the click in his knee as a wrong he has done.
Eight is the sound of someone listening who is too far to hear.
Ninth is the sound of this list being written.

On Wednesday the black X in the Sunday box is the tenant
    next door
three days from now obeying an X she had drawn,
or else hoping that while she lay sleeping
a fire might start in the next room over.

On Thursday the black X in the Sunday box is no good for
    thinking people
ever think of other people
and the cigarettes they neglect in sleep.

On Friday the black X in the Sunday box insists on rules for
    rules,
positions the furniture to look certain
about the conditions, certain codes of conduct
decreed by the room itself.

On Saturday the black X in the Sunday box is a black X in a
    Sunday box:
the mark on a map for a thing safely buried.

The Balance

A single blue stocking in one hand
in my other a man

with a wooden cross nailed to his limbs.
Which hand weighs the most?

Does redemption weigh more
than two weaves of blue?

Does blood painted on
weigh more than a stain?

Did walking her here
and sweat on the way

push down on the blue
and up on the man?

Can a run that begins in the arch
weigh more than a gash?

Do prayers weigh more
than a moan that was heard?

Is it the missing hill
or the shape a leg leaves behind?

Will forgiveness weigh more
than a weight taken off?

This is the Color

This is the color even God wants nothing to do with.
On the scraped side of his turned-away face,
when dying this color is what you'll see last.

This is the god even nothing wants nothing to do with.
A god forever sulking in the shadow of his hood
hates most of all to be your thoughts.

This is creation scribbled between corners—
each moment another exponent
piling up behind God's first regret.

This is the dust from the sawed-off half of the moon
settling on the face of a man who smokes in bed.
There are so many days he can't remember.

These are the men who die in public.
Whose ravens get sent for and peck by decree.
You sold your first lie to one of these men.

And this knife carving the word *Love*.
Found in the pockets of every dead soldier,
nothing one word will not do to another.

On the Dangers of Not Reading Aloud

Each intrusion was bound in weather.
The outline of the desired scale was often
scored by weather, meaning the flesh side
of the outlined intrusion came fringed
with regrets tasseled together.
Some regrets consisted of rain.
To this was added a psalm—
hummingbirds over the book.
Rain was a lance taken from the book.
Rain was to protect a book.
And sunlight to keep it closed.
That is to say a single page of weather
folded down the center intrudes upon the book.
Though in sunlight rain is supplanted by two smaller psalms.
Rain psalms gape at the head.
They tire heedlessly
and intrude on the mist leaving the head.

On the Dangers of Reading Alone

This would seem confirmed
by the vendors of duplicate weather.
Although no one season envisions
the same two brothers.
Nor is there agreement.

Do gradations of haze,
with but one exception, reflect the same
book twice? This one exception
would seem to me crimping haze
from my brother's buried hand.

It offers almost seaponds of wording
and yet gradation was discarded.
It was my brother's buried hand recording a word.
Together with a few opening pages of weather,
he endures the last pages of weather.

And a book to be discarded
without crippling the weather.

On the Dangers of Reading for Sound

The self-begotten seed has yet to inform you.
To assure you it slaves to be visible. Barbelo
the Virgin presides in the seed, the fields,
and the missing who travel in spheres
of their own accord. They did happen.
Same way the aspirant lingers towards
goodness (ordinary sounds are good, though
prevented from revealing the whole topic),
they wait to proceed in glades that appear,
in glades they appear as seen from afar
and yearn to know sounds of dual-time value.

By means of beat and pitch they submit
to the orders—silence and impulse.
Among the first sounds (some are less
and they submit to the orders) a few divide
into man and woman (intermediates
for resembling each other) *bagadazatha,*
zethe, and now *ogadozotho*—you shall
collect them and without apparatus.
Now as is the purpose of sound,
go forth and separate the angels.

There will be some effects which are good
for they are in need of their own shape: one
and two resemble nothing, they are first
to exist. Whereas three (being divided)
belongs to the guess-work of saving,
four is received by the weather
and on the weather's tetravalent winds
four is received.
Six reigns alone, perfected by six.

Hebdomadal receives beauty already born into the weather.
Into the weather Hebdomadal sleeps, her armor of gongs
quilted together. And when the octaves are ready
the whole place is set free into weather.
But eleven and twelve grew restless traversing the seams.
They grew honest, but through means of separation.
They pitted marks upon a point and the whole place
is pitted with sound. Thus do sounds that are good
exist in separation.

Paradise: *Directions for Reading*

Act One

Begin by grinding your beaks out loud to the world.
Huddle together like seeds in a bowl.
Leave the husks and fields behind.
Take care to wince.

Scene One

Perform this part with an arc of irritation.
Read the stage instructions as if they were
instructions for the stage itself.
Lose your place and make clever comments
about the lost place you thought was mine.

Scene Two

Suppose you could all stand in line
and care less about the line.
Pretend you're competing against the tenderness
the line feels for itself.
Allow for private dismays of affection.
If on account of its own self-knowledge
the line begins to slither,
feel free to let it slither
up and down the aisles.
Allow it to coil in on itself.
At the players where the rings overlap

have them step out and make assessments.
Imagine all scenarios have been exhausted.
Don a collective face.
Feel it oscillate
between lewd and blameless faces.

Scene Three

Surrender yourself to an incident.
Say you met an incident while waiting at Gate 22.
Say you made secret love to the incident.
Now cast her out beneath the benches of the terminal.
Write it in the margins.
Have the extras write it too.

Intermission

Suspend a black box for every one who'd rather not.

Act Two

Get involved with the audience.
Tell them one of your secrets. Have them act it out.
Tell them to act like their parents.
Tell them all to wear nothing but sashes.
Tell them you are a certain food,
not a group, but a kind of food that won't belong.
Tell them to chew along to the music.

Scene One

Read this part as if the lighting
were more important than the text itself.
Occasionally stop in mid-sentence
to make flustered adjustments.
Program a series of bulbs
to blink out a sequence of varied blues.
Say you feel bad about having to start over.
Start over without disguising
the pride you have in starting over.
By now all save the soloist
should feel safely hidden behind their gowns.
Naked, she whirls about the stage.
She whirls with the air of someone
who doesn't want to be whirling.
She seems worried for her self.
Her movements are at once graceful and cloopy,
and yet without the excuse of dancing naked.

Scene Two

Read this part from memory
even though your gaze remains fixed on the page.
Invent succinct little gestures that indicate
when someone other than the speaker is speaking.
"In this part there is a cacophony of speakers."
Say it, proud of your tendency to boast about parts.
Alert the audience to a glossary
of gestures at the back of their programs.
Allow enough time for fluency.
Begin reading and making up new gestures.
Substitute alien gestures for each gesture so assigned.

Eventually do away with gestures all together.
Begin speaking with no voice at all.
Stand there, silent and secretly gestured—
affect an armless voice in search for itself.

Scene Three

Admire the set of your own design.
Spread out your wings—
your most elegant narrator's glide.
Observe how the down inside
is scalloped with judgment.
See crenels that flap at the wind.
Flap at the wind.
Now perch there and sing yourself a day.
Begin pecking at every soul not selected.

The Fourth Book of Nathan

Today my fourth book of Nathan
is a black calf and a slowness
led out for dragging the pasture behind.
Born already old, deliberate,
with head low to the ground,
the book survives in a time left for grass.
The grass, ample and for now
lacking the blackness of the calf,
grows for dying beautifully.
In a blue dress I wear to go wishing
I hid forty-two pages folded in squares.
Nathan wants me alone with the paper.
Says I'm no good at lying
and that I keep turning over.
He calls me "Summer." Says
I'm a summer we can sleep through.

Adam Collects Himself

Once, our cries came already broken.
Came part way down until the all night stranded circle
gleamed with the threat of sweat knowing itself.
And for reasons no seer could see,
even the pewter-sheen cat-saucer dip in her hip
exists because I would not look away.

But now my kingdom,
she is cast out like corners in a room.
And where there are voices (not ours,
dying at stations far off in the flesh),
they come to speak on behalf of the room,
come to lace the mistrust they hold for each other,
with the mixture of dust we took for ourselves.

My love always lacked truthfulness —
I could not love without fearing her death.
And yet I longed to love unknowingly,
without God, which is the revenge
of those who know.

Circled Square Drawn to Scale

The wisdom of the square lies in the way
it boasts three times about its first lie told
and asserts around every corner
its own confessed greed for space—

how else and more completely
could it hate itself the most?
When every clock masquerades
as a square not taking place.

Even in the most well-rounded towns
where they exact a square and perhaps a fountain,
where always two sets of people walk there in twos,
save just a few who stand to the side

selecting the ones that get lined
up against the walls
in a smattering that consoles
what three clean walls remain.

There blood settles in pools, proof enough.
To exceed ourselves we've tried every angle.
Why else would a square makes us bleed
from the side of us all?

Is the cross a square in crisis,
endlessly open to the possibility
of at least one man who won't
contain God's love?

Or just an old square finally showing its shards.
Not the claw of the crowd,
but the tracks from the crowd
clawing its way

towards where each and every square
forgives the supreme shame of shape.
O sing me of death in one line
and I'll die you a death in four.

Not Taking Place

Now all I see are orange circles
arousing themselves against a high pylon
of days.

In the first place
we have no place else to go,
and in the second, we've aligned ourselves
behind the protective malaise
of our amazement—

an old haze rising
on a day that makes amends
by making every day that follows

the inside of all the broken circles,
where construction on the orange ones
must beg to begin—

where shards from a chipped tooth are ground into powder
and rubbed with design along the outside rims,

rims that mimic the trembling eyelid of God,
a god that pleads "No, no ... not in my sleep ..."
then sends ripples across the waters of his own device—

ripples turn into waves
consuming the villages
where bowls get made.

Though it's no catastrophe
when I cut my lip on the edge,
when drops of blood splatter the page

drying in orange circles
that keep the page from turning.

Because There is No Soft

If the moon is not yet looked upon, the moon is not yet askance,
not yet without itself, but a long way looking back,
back to when there are no people, but weren't there always
    dead people
entrusting their encampments to the inside of yellow?

Want a face that blows back at the wind?
Won't a face blow the wind back?

See a man all broken in threes.
At this hour his horse of changing names.
It is so much sweating out beads that gleam with the look of
    your face.
It is enamored and disarmed by the cold dross of day.

Because there is no soft gusting through bones,
nor beam of light that once preceded—
just a stick man without his three reasons,
just a stick man who gives up on his tree.

Lord, I have looked out and seen myself,
seen how the shade in the reason is yellow.
It is a shade without itself, it is without
reason, burned down and in some parts
still burning.

November

I grew wind behind the orchard.
Behind the oxbow I grew wind.

Took some doing behind your house—

clay contracted with rain,
a rain it wouldn't carry,
now even the roots tumble away.

Wind, where will you cease to
and how will you mention yourself to the cold?

At night I wonder what to do.

This winter knows
where I've been living.

Bulrushes

The clear offspring of last people appears at my door.

There is a day old gash in the side of the basket
and a note I will not read.

One thinks I should cling to an apostrophe of people.

Those were the days in one sitting.
Nothing can happen in a cream-colored conversation.

"You're welcome," she said, though I still was not born.

Nettles

Blue-grey hairs misinform like an aura,
like a clenched halo serrated by jays
might exorcise pain out from its seeming
deflected till next year's calcitrant lawn.
Nettles seldom waver into the air,
nor do they buttress as lilies will do—
our slovenly sighs asleep in their tents.
How many javelins blunted in violet
pierce open the spheres relieved of their dead?
In violet we spire above what purpose
the rest of heaven can only portend.

Blue

All the unseated blue in the world.
Some concessions for blue.
How blue flakes away into blue.
The aging of blue.
Dismissed cravings of blue.
And nothing so remote as a blue.
The penchant in blue insisting on blue.
Daisies are blue.
Blue in between when nothing will come.
The blue pulse in a lie.
Rifts.
This solvent is blue.

On the Resemblance Distinguished from Others

The first few days
are the smallest.
In spite of the way
they're assembled
(according to the means
of all the days that follow)
they possess a different
gleam and burn for reasons
purely sacrificial.
A single day
dismembered for days
passes over
with the look of any other.

Siphons

The mouth pressed to her lectern of waters.
The face conceding its features.
The tongue that also concedes.
Plans for a reef pending in secret.
The break one can feel implying the reef.
And when the sea opens to a breath that was held,
her own blue vaulted breath.
Skin on a mountain embarking for sea.
The skin on a mountain.

Wilderness

A forkful of rain held over your tongue.
A rack where the desert can land.
My tented field of a free and open nature.
Water according to your own due surface.
Of clay already pitted with me.

I gave you my fulcrum.
I gave you her sleep.
A bed with everything present.
Let the bruised summer palace resemble a cloud.
Let dune palm ladle your death.

Put them scraping together.
Divine them where the willow is cut.
Do as my haste trade them for shell.
You can have languid.
You can have dusk.

Central Square

With this one kiss I now accept the modern city.
It was the time your hair already sparkling.
An unusual gentle shape—suppose I relented
each *where will I be without thee?* and devout hairs
shine in the mouth like tears bathing a street.
Yes, I now accept the modern city, I accept its everydayness.
I accept catalogs for holiday candy need to be clearly
    conceived,
and bins for commingled containers color-coded for days.
I accept there are days, like precincts not fully counted,
and that some nights can pass in the space of a window.
There are windows with decals and decals the hand
with solvent tries to avoid ... Let another
sing for the lapidary, and another burn heretical burns.
From the window with deep spoons a street lamp offers your
    breast.
Tonight will I take you without seeing your breast?
Spine like a staircase, leave me astray.

A *Third* Tree

It was I and not all the world who took the blow
from his ambient seizure. Like promise, like death
without meaning, like he came with always frank and sullen
precision and now off with some new need fulfilling my trance.
I was skilled at the moans and not just my last one
took up with his truly. *Wilderness*—the very word made us go wild
and feel like an island sang for the sea. For high tide I thought
all the figures and when I parcel paint on his shoulders,
I martial tribes on the rocks. There was always some way,
and this way the dust excites till the end. O we had sunrises
and such natural effects as a cowbell and wood violets
comprising the quiet. Where it put love to sleep I saw no good
reason proceeding and the death mask gardens can be.
Ours was always one part collision, two parts roam, and not even
this hurled city corrupts our all time fuchsia.   ❧

Oubliette

The thought of my violin sonata
jangles on a wagon asleep with the places.
Sleep accepts this place slightly created.
Modicums do war beyond the places.
About their objectives it has nothing to say—
there exist three shades of love.
As if wondering, they follow the wagon
up through the helpless mountain.
A fourth shade laggards behind,
a lurch for the wagon I drew.
She looks to be mist regarding its plume.
Mist feeds on the rays dead to the gazer below.
He can hear shade taking shape from a hole,
not procedures of shade strung to the hole.

Io

Night almost no longer fallen
and the agony of somehow
dismantles the wood. Shape
and the gladness of verdure
fan out, surrounded by ways.
One way is homely
and wanders off to a life
her mother intends.
Another is already taken.
Another covered in leaves.
And this way mentioned in time.
This way for song fleck and the refugee
whispers of two people who shouldn't.
She shouldn't whisper the coves.
So shouldn't want to fill her with boats.
Not like infinity, like the endless
inside her one other mouth.

Shutesbury

There is one time, and one time
with a hillside passing through.

Grass was a method
and one time pretend a hissing wetness,
pretend tumbling
and the mountains you can tell

how I held the wind from all the world
and one time because of clover
and one time because of rye
and the bracelet I was learning
to make out of grasses,

hung loose like a seafloor,
hung without trying, dryness or towns,
and one town because of sleep
and in one town I saw her dress
with a band of sunlight passing through.

Today is two bits of human figment,
and one kiss because of sound—
a cool sleep on the hill
came down careening.

Which Oval Her Ministry

Which oval her ministry sought to ignore
depends on the crown she reneges
back to when cushions (dimples despondent)
suggest a rescinded corsage.
She decrees three ovals crushed inside another
might impact the flowers I shove
out past the dune eluded for days, we constrict
all the way blue into begun.
All the way blue into begun, teach me the circles
that erstwhile over the surf
a light to confide in. Light from her scepter
(some divers mistake it for depth)
bores past the seafloor cataracting with ovals.

Clear Blue Kite

Your clear blue kite
everlasting into the elm.
Often not saying this
my branches wait
unnoticed in danger.
A sick elm impending
the other with sickness.
Or a bleached kite
shred for the child who fell.
I have fallen where no dress
can make me feel older.
Even this black one
I unzip with the snow.

The Drawstring Hisses

could one intonate the gown of passing near
from the gown of passing by
my own gown would cast this cast-out ragged hue
clear beyond concession or settle for the sounds
I hear the soprano half of my insolence
request from the nudes
fanning out to a shrill
gossamer shrill and forbidden to fold
some mornings it garlands into a moan
the drawstring hisses *let the diary speak for itself*
if you want you can hurt it
it wants to conceive
and thins to a fragrance some blue light
burns in the banister's sheen
the mist
the crumpled hour
the hand-in-hand with wandering
and all their solitary ways ran out to greet us

In Between Jed and Yeul

Whereas during place to place encounters
the clenching response is given by crooned
I-give-you-away movements, suggesting
I may kiss you at times for any length
and the historical fact of having been
led through so tight a hoop of encloudment.
Jed notes latent changes in a perfume.
Yeul intones a ghost-ship where the hen
nods piously about the dead, for they
have no appetite—yet both would allow
for ordinate time to prey on the mouth
the third person implies more directly.
There are too many of us, each soaring
from the ray startled mesa of our groans,
to the soft green waters—inadvertent,
like the hue crown in mattering late,
or the signals inferred during our sleep.

Dear Uriah

As it is the union of two
separate wills, a great deal
of elsewhere inhabits our bed.

I had wanted a canopy
of all things Uriah.
In place I got Time, all three

of his tongues tolling within.
One tongue—clear and thick
with everlasting the bath.

Another is rail thin and leaves me
covered in droves. But a third
tongue pressing on like a wedge

through elsewhere's demise ...
O it hurts like some day
there are no other days.

Hurts like *further*—
like a tongue
the first time can't deserve.

Castrovalva

That I could learn the sponding crevices
a woman has taken me into her mouth.
Full spectrums of midwife size differences
grow braided together and into a crevice.
I can see there's a crevice for everything—
a crevice for stagecraft, a crevice for yolk.
Take each particular fleck
on her long fluted dress cut from the straps
and strewn by the wind of its hisses,
still I can see the crevices
sponding inside perfectly,
like sun rays sponding a lake.

Elegy for Music

Her mouth was also a sledge to carry me twice
up pastures of flatness to hills where I lay
now dead to the world and some clouds that I miss
are more infinitely apt to cling to the crags,
to think when they sag—ours is a pale activity
compared to the wanderings that pass for a man,
to his ink washed pages all pining to be,
now less than a wetness, now less than a glare,
in light of this pass no timber can breach,
in light of this woman who happened too fast,
and while she sleeps with a green hand under the earth
how can we lean out from our sacks?
and why should we silver our failed versions of sound?
when the softest among us is wintering down.

Warning Bretagne

From her problem shoulder
I see daring little corsets
bobbing in the moat.

I can wash myself in all
the hand-bitten mirrors
flicking from her tower.

Defender of lesser things,
even the seashell watches
over her shoulder.

Seashell listen to me —
hair without cunning
O hairs of creation.

Hand under hand
I climb down one of you
corrupting the hiss.

Fingers

One finger secrets a hill.
Another slinks past a watchtower
blazing off into sleep.
A third lies face down,
a face prospecting the sea.
Some sea, but not before hushing the world.
And this finger won't betray for the world.
No one can see it, let nobody see.

Tear Garden

Your cabinet is a long time coming.
Light in your house has an outside swollen hue.
At night speechlessness happens.
There were many balls, they speckle your body.
What day did you come down from?

Hornet

You look to be heavy with children
separately carried in imminent space.
In the distance your head is positioned
lengthwise and in the future tense,

when the helmet surrenders to bliss,
death to the fiction of speed.
August barge of the air
you look to be taking on water

and with a gunmetal straw
the prophesied way to my room—
this way for trumpets muffled in yellow
this way for sleep segmented with sleep.

It frightens me that your stinger
is so set off by itself—held,
but at a distance, as when drilling
a gong, or conducting a flare.

Rose Maker's Fever

Monstrosities of two minds regulate the Rose—
parallel circumstance with human kind,
and their particular vision of Holy Dread.

No species of thinking seems worthy of Since.
Since—*no trellis is wretched* ...
No trellis begins by waxing a plan.

Never descends below the consultation of pleasure,
Nor, the embattled ark of your illness—
where the garment gapes the body ignites.

The greater part of Time begins at the mouth.
Decorate disguises with Time—
it is a common auditor who wishes you won't.

Whoever had qualities alarming the trellis,
emulates Love before the Rose can inflame.

Whereas calamity hovers over the victims of Should,
the Rose pays early, its anguish is barren.
Mine can't deserve the kindness of thorns.

Visible grace begins at the head.
At the head some other fondness lay open.
It remarks on the slightness of day,

for while the scabbard boasts rarely of day,
the Lord is lavish with day.
Like a rose, it must be provoked.

On the Conditions Presently Needed

Each having something to say and the insolence to say it,
the future is a sore-spot between the past and present.
While one demands her husband be buried in the front lawn,
another wanders in the hall, wondering *but I'm not even dead.*
There, their son Future—forever finding and hiding the shovel.

One day the shovel unearths a day of its own.
Suddenly there are lips in the way it looks at things.
The earth seems fine just as it lays.
There's more than enough holes already,
of these the sky is not to be confused,
worried and desperate, caves in the sky.

Ragged: the sky is nothing more than the collective rage of holes.
Today: the shovel sends all the birds that respond to a shovel.
Tomorrow: not a single bird alights to piece the holes together.

These are the conditions Presently needed.
The men are important but without the grim
splendor of a day in ruin it just won't happen.

Who said men?
It's really only boys
who come to call out her name.

Who said boys? Really it's only one
who stands naked to the clothes
she drapes over the chair.

Moonlight dapples his face
Arms wooden for resting
O the sounds a boy can make

Who said sounds?
The room is forever empty of boys.
She both heard and said the sounds.

Boy for Sale

I once new a builder of sunken ships whose patch was horrible
                    but the eye it hid was even worse.

On still nights he held me close pointing to a wrecked sky he
                    said he built himself.

Behind the ditched salt-truck is where a boy's first star-milk
                    begins to leak.

When the two of us ran off together he ran off with someone
                    else.

Closing my eyes, I can still see the painted lips that took my
place, the black stockings spread out like spider webs, like a
                    dark delicious grid.

Now this wooden overcoat hurts to wear and a smaller rain
                    hurts most of all.

Now all the drowned sailors hate me and the living ones cover
                    me with oil.

Both float up, always face-down, mouthing my name.

I'm still fine to lie down with, though when their ships are
                    christened they send me away.

From my hiding place they don't know I can still hex a vessel or
                    from this far curse the calmest sea.

I never hold a shell and hear his wet kiss pounding me slowly.

I never walk the waterfront wearing the tight dress designed by
gulls.

I never see the night sky, his overlapping patches.

I never call his name. Never in the half-light do I cry myself to
sleep.

The sea is a green circle with my feet tied to the edges.

The Sea Looking On

The shoreline has always obeyed
and one day permission was given to me.

I was only one swimmer and I swam to be told—
a slow mist and light from the far house chrysanthemum-sad.

I swam to see my thin troubled sister asleep on the floor,
the current and creatures exploring her hair,

and possibly a moon down from the surface she no longer
believes.

Who can tell her lips from the coral, sleep from the spray,
and when the sea shifts waves high above practice her name.

But for the breakers I could not find her.
Only the coiled password for breathing picked at and spoken.

Had I only been there to say it between us.
Had only I painted her once without water,

just once without paint and the sea looking on.

The Moon is a Moon

What is it about the moon that makes it fall onto so many pages.
Hauled down by eyes netted together.
You who made the moon small by the hugeness of it all,
ask of the moon to be more than a moon.

The moon is not a pickled ghost,
nor a face swollen beneath some giant leap.
The moon is not your mother,
nor a bucket of breath longing to breathe.

The moon is not a hole
into an alternative sky
where the dark is quiet,
the thunder white.

The moon not shining
its own light to shine,
not a reservoir thought up
for the storage of lakes,

or where a reserve of hidden people
worships collision.
And the moon is not the whisper from all the dark places,
whispering "I'm sorry for all the dark places."

The moon is a rock with blue scrapes.

The Bird Maker's Last

Few birds have been so arduous as this present dove.
For one reason, it does not feel the Lord is trusted.
And my last three passed without meaning—
from such noises and corruptions of spirit
that I find it tiresome to create even ordinary finches.

But if I trust the weakens arising from chores
knows an aspect of God and the fatigue of his labor
(palpable, and with the resolve of future makers),
perhaps this dove enables my hands
to shuffle spaces with Time, causation with Grace,
and on the walls of her tower my hands crawl around,
hapless, and with the lewd pretense of instructing each other.

Up here the wind is wanting
and my hands think I have little.
For if the Lord wishes me to be a bird
let his Majesty retract the birds
and be pleased to recall my obedience
and the haste I took in his service.

The devil's aim cannot be lightly taken—
he is trying to bring about a cooling of love
and not the arbors in a late night
construed for their roost.
Or can his shrewd perfections only be God
observing the trials my bird-making brings?

Who else begins with a blackened dove?
I fear it must be a reluctant emblem.
It must be Hesitation—a long time
when no one occurs.

Dawn

Continuing, we came upon the third prospect of shelves
    carved like cradles into the side of the cliff.
    The fear in us wonders if the infants were removed,

or rather tapered off, neglecting cribs of their own.
    Dhorsen, the first to step up and begin blowing dust,
    and as the dust rose in twin fitful, lascivious clouds,

it seemed as though Dhorsen was no longer with us,
    Dhorsen was no longer with us, but with a head
    depicted as Wind, his lips grew old, bulbous

and from here on pushing fair-weather and now
    disaster up past our somnolent map-maker's
    seafaring corner ...

This far low the next day returns to a face,
    and with lineaments hooded with powder,
    scars labeled "sleek and approaching,"

the next day came and with the same blended facets as on a
        man ...
    No, with only his profile, storm-drained and caked with
        tomorrows,
    Dhorsen turned, still tending his circuit of cribs—

"We must learn to limit our choices," and as one
    whose voice rises from the radius of Nil, one
    whose throat welters at no other circle, Dhorsen turned

and made the motion for us to blow in his manner …
    When done was done, when each felt they'd disturbed
    more dust than his fellow, instead of citing Abduction,

or the spurious rumors of cradles foregone, we saw how
    the missing infants, before growing old, first prattled
    "layers of sepulcher" for us to pond.

And though our mothers are no longer with us
    (though I know her plangent sounds kept records for Nil),
    we each held a mother, sleepy in pages and pages

of no other place …
    Continuing, we came upon the third prospect of shelves
    carved like cradles into the side of the cliff

Orso began weeping, confessing, and splashing his paints
    on the cribs we had taken. Orso always begins
    weeping and referring to verities hidden inside.

I remember how in the first rank precincts of Ellipsis,
    Orso begged us to study his braid. Poor Orso, with his
    side-winding frown and penchant for kissing,

longs for us all to settle our loves. I remember how
    in the first rank precincts of Ellipsis,
    Orso begged us to churn like a rose.

Poor Orso, with his sidereal gown and fist full of love-nots,
    prefers moonlight and Deference dragged by the hair …
    Continuing, we came upon the third prospect of shelves

carved like cradles into the side of the cliff.
    While the hailed pretext of Wheel still hung above our heads,
    the impostor pursuing us seemed no longer fatal.

At the Crib's behest, we each grew no longer monstrous,
    no longer bad, and the day absolves in tones of hesitation.
    None of us tremble as only the guilty will tremble,

but revolve in hues and our three tints braid together.
    Behold, the banners advance—
    how easily black banners change into wings ...

But I'm sad for a lantern that keeps dawn at bay.
    I'm Dawn, moving up on a list of fallen things.
    I don't want to be dark, the dark that concedes,

and I beg to differ the sly part of gentle.
    I beg for the day I rise in the morning.
    I beg in the morning—Orso,

Dhorsen, grant me your leave.
    Mine is a poor light
    and glad to be

continuing

Notes

"My Death Bed of Flowers" is for Tomaz Salamun.

"On the Dangers of Reading for Sound" is built within and around the lacunae found in the Gnostic text *Marsanes*. The words *bagadazatha*, *zethe*, and *bogadozotho* are theurgic vowel-consonant combinations used in ritual chant and thought to aid the soul in ascent.

"Oubliette" is for Matthew Zapruder, who suggested its title.

"Shutesbury" is for Holly Spaulding.

"Which Oval Her Ministry" owes a debt to Ed O'Connell who alerted me to the rhyme scheme in James Merrill's poem "The Octopus," from which it borrows.

"Castrovalva" takes its title from a drawing by M.C. Escher.

About the Author

Peter Richards was born in Urbana, Illinois in 1967. His honors include an Iowa Arts Fellowship, The John Logan Award, an Academy of American Poets Prize, and a Massachusetts Cultural Council Artist Grant in Poetry. He teaches at Tufts University and lives in Somerville, Massachusetts. *Oubliette* is his first book.